D1389097

I love
you to the
Moon
and back

summersdale

I LOVE YOU TO THE MOON AND BACK

First published in 2014

This edition copyright © Summersdale Publishers Ltd, 2016

Summersdale Publishers Ltd
46 West Street
Chichester
West Sussex
PO19 1RP
UK

www.summersdale.com

Printed and bound in China

ISBN: 978-1-84953-918-0

Substantial discounts on bulk quantities of Summersdale books are available to corporations, professional associations and other organisations. For details contact Nicky Douglas by telephone: +44 (0) 1243 756902, fax: +44 (0) 1243 786300 or email: nicky@summersdale.com.

To.....................................

From.................................

*Love*
*knows not distance;*
*it hath no continent;*
*its eyes are*
*for the stars...*

Gilbert Parker

Talk not of wasted affection; affection never was wasted.

Henry Wadsworth Longfellow

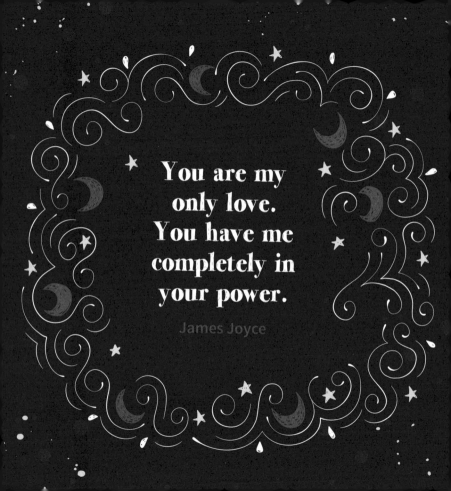

You are my
only love.
You have me
completely in
your power.

James Joyce

YOU COME TO LOVE
NOT BY FINDING
THE PERFECT PERSON,
BUT BY SEEING
AN IMPERFECT
PERSON PERFECTLY.

Sam Keen

LOVE IS BUT THE
DISCOVERY OF
OURSELVES IN OTHERS,
AND THE DELIGHT IN
THE RECOGNITION.

Alexander Smith

O come, and
take from me
The pain of being
deprived of thee!

Thomas Campion

If I had a flower
for every time
I thought of
you... I could
walk through my
garden forever.

**Alfred, Lord Tennyson**

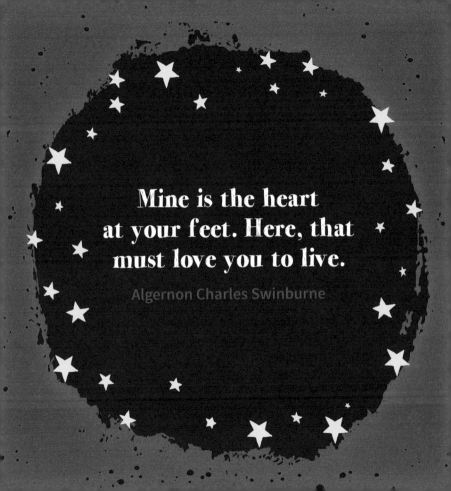

Mine is the heart
at your feet. Here, that
must love you to live.

Algernon Charles Swinburne

Love recognises no barriers. It jumps hurdles, leaps fences, penetrates walls to arrive at its destination full of hope.

Maya Angelou

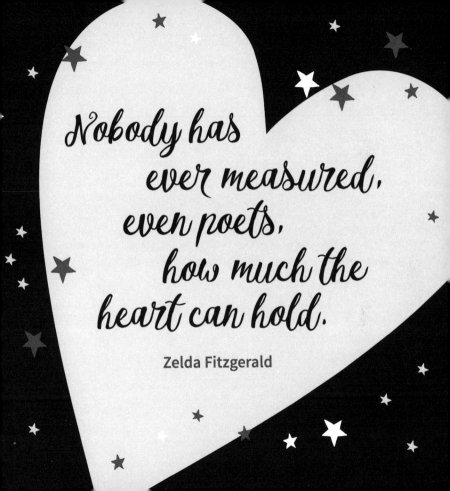

Nobody has ever measured, even poets, how much the heart can hold.

Zelda Fitzgerald

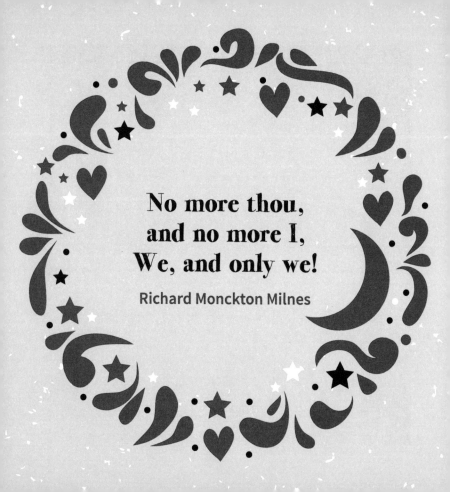

No more thou,
and no more I,
We, and only we!

Richard Monckton Milnes

YOU HAVE MADE A
PLACE IN MY HEART
WHERE I THOUGHT
THERE WAS NO ROOM
FOR ANYTHING ELSE.

**Robert Jordan**

# There is always some madness in love. But there is also some reason in madness.

Friedrich Nietzsche

She is the heart
that strikes
a whole octave.
After her all
songs are possible.

Rainer Maria Rilke

One word frees
us of all the
weight and pain
of life:
that word is love.

Sophocles

In love
the paradox occurs
that two beings
become one
and yet
remain two.

Erich Fromm

Love is in all
things a most
wonderful teacher.

Charles Dickens

WE ARE ALL BORN
FOR LOVE... IT IS
THE PRINCIPLE OF
EXISTENCE, AND
ITS ONLY END.

Benjamin Disraeli

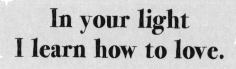

**In your light
I learn how to love.**

Rumi

O my Luve's
like a red, red rose,
That's newly
sprung in June.

Robert Burns

The madness
of love is the
greatest
of heaven's
blessings.

Plato

A loving heart is
the beginning of
all knowledge.

Thomas Carlyle

WHEN I SAW
YOU I FELL IN
LOVE. AND YOU
SMILED BECAUSE
YOU KNEW.

**Arrigo Boito**

Love
vanquishes
time.

Mary Parrish

If thou hadst never
met mine eye,
I had not dreamed
a living face
Could fancied
charms so far
outvie.

Anne Brontë

Anyone
can be passionate,
but it takes
real lovers
to be silly.

Rose Franken

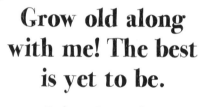

**Grow old along with me! The best is yet to be.**

Robert Browning

My love, my hope,
my all shall be,
To look to heaven
and look to thee!

William Winter

*The best thing to hold on to in life is each other.*

Audrey Hepburn

**Love must be as much a light as a flame.**

Henry David Thoreau

**Soul meets soul
on lovers' lips.**

Percy Bysshe Shelley

# Love is friendship set on fire.

Jeremy Taylor

EVENTUALLY YOU WILL
COME TO UNDERSTAND
THAT LOVE HEALS
EVERYTHING, AND
LOVE IS ALL THERE IS.

**Gary Zukav**

Come live
in my
heart,
and pay no rent.

Samuel Lover

I AM IN LOVE –
AND, MY GOD,
IT'S THE GREATEST
THING THAT CAN
HAPPEN TO A MAN.

D. H. Lawrence

LOVE IS A GAME
THAT TWO CAN
PLAY AND
BOTH WIN

**Eva Gabor**

# A heart that loves is always young.

**Greek proverb**

WE WERE
TOGETHER —
ALL ELSE HAS
LONG BEEN
FORGOTTEN
BY ME.

**Walt Whitman**

In dreams and in love there are no impossibilities.

János Arany

**Paradise is always where love dwells.**

Jean Paul

One half
of me is yours,
the other
half yours.

William Shakespeare

EACH MOMENT
OF A HAPPY
LOVER'S HOUR IS
WORTH AN AGE
OF DULL AND
COMMON LIFE.

Aphra Behn

I love her and that's the beginning and end of everything.

F. Scott Fitzgerald

# Love does not dominate; it cultivates.

**Johann Wolfgang von Goethe**

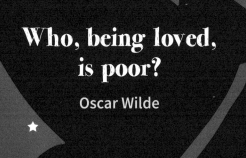

Who, being loved,
is poor?

Oscar Wilde

NOTHING WE DO,
HOWEVER VIRTUOUS,
CAN BE ACCOMPLISHED
ALONE; THEREFORE WE
ARE SAVED BY LOVE.

Reinhold Niebuhr

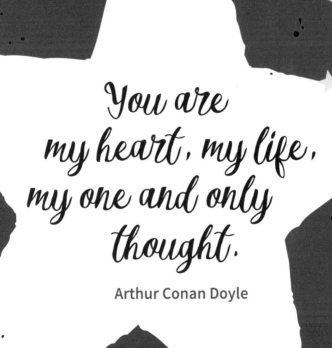

You are
my heart, my life,
my one and only
thought.

Arthur Conan Doyle

# With thee conversing I forget all time.

John Milton

# THE WINDS WERE WARM ABOUT US, THE WHOLE EARTH SEEMED THE WEALTHIER FOR OUR LOVE.

Harriet Elizabeth Prescott Spofford

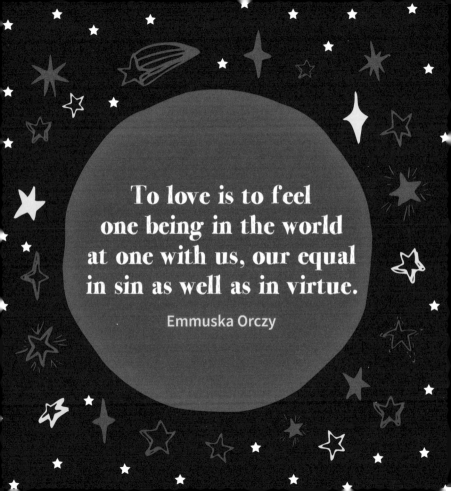

To love is to feel
one being in the world
at one with us, our equal
in sin as well as in virtue.

Emmuska Orczy

Love is the
only gold.

Alfred, Lord Tennyson

Love is of all passions the strongest, for it attacks simultaneously the head, the heart and the senses.

Lao Tzu

Love in its
essence is
spiritual fire.

Emanuel Swedenborg

WHERE THERE IS
LOVE THERE IS
NO QUESTION.

**Albert Einstein**

Love conquers all
things; let us too
surrender to love.

Virgil

Love is the beauty
of the soul.

Augustine of Hippo

THE BEST AND MOST
BEAUTIFUL THINGS...
CANNOT BE SEEN
OR EVEN HEARD,
BUT MUST BE FELT
WITH THE HEART.

Helen Keller

We love because
it is the only
true adventure.

Nikki Giovanni

And looking to the Heaven, that bends above you, How oft! I bless the lot that made me love you.

Samuel Taylor Coleridge

LOVE DOESN'T MAKE
THE WORLD GO ROUND
LOVE IS WHAT MAKES
THE RIDE WORTHWHILE

**Franklin P. Jones**

And in the convulsive
rapture of a kiss –
Thus doth love speak.

Ella Wheeler Wilcox

ROMANCE IS THE GLAMOUR WHICH TURNS THE DUST OF EVERYDAY LIFE INTO A GOLDEN HAZE.

Elinor Glyn

Love is everything
it's cracked up to
be... It really is worth
fighting for. Being
brave for, risking
everything for.

Erica Jong

Two souls with
but a single thought,
two hearts that
beat as one.

Friedrich Halm

I HAVE SPREAD MY
DREAMS UNDER
YOUR FEET;
TREAD SOFTLY
BECAUSE YOU TREAD
ON MY DREAMS.

W. B. Yeats

Doubt thou the stars are fire;
Doubt that the sun doth move;
Doubt truth to be a liar;
But never doubt I love.

**William Shakespeare**

**There is no remedy
for love
but to love more.**

Henry David Thoreau

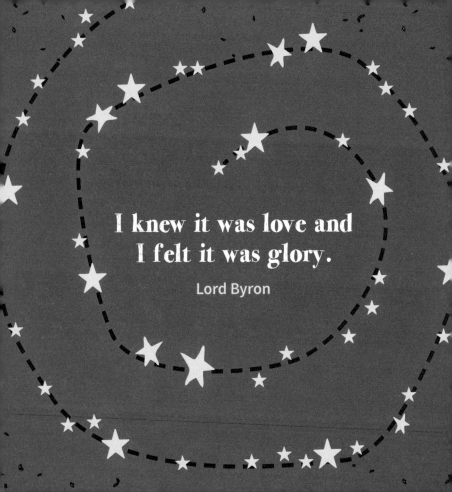

I knew it was love and
I felt it was glory.

Lord Byron

Love has
no uttermost,
as the stars
have no number
and the sea
no rest.

Eleanor Farjeon

LOVE IS AN INDESCRIBABLE SENSATION — PERHAPS A CONVICTION, A SENSE OF CERTITUDE.

Joyce Carol Oates

**Love is being
stupid together.**

Paul Valéry

THE GREATEST HAPPINESS
OF LIFE IS THE
CONVICTION THAT WE
ARE LOVED – LOVED
FOR OURSELVES, OR
RATHER, LOVED IN
SPITE OF OURSELVES.

**Victor Hugo**

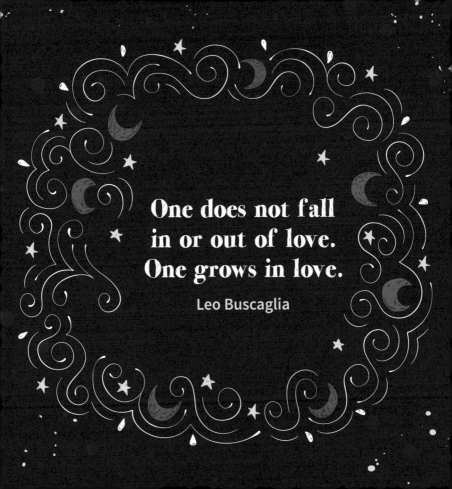

One does not fall
in or out of love.
One grows in love.

Leo Buscaglia

In our life there is
a single colour…
which provides the
meaning of life
and art. It is the
colour of love.

Marc Chagall

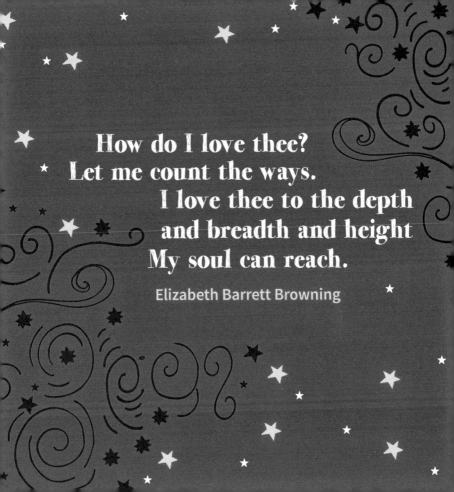

How do I love thee?
Let me count the ways.
I love thee to the depth
and breadth and height
My soul can reach.

Elizabeth Barrett Browning

I carry your heart with me
(I carry it in my heart).

E. E. Cummings

LOVE IS SOMETHING
ETERNAL ; THE ASPECT
MAY CHANGE, BUT
NOT THE ESSENCE.

Vincent van Gogh

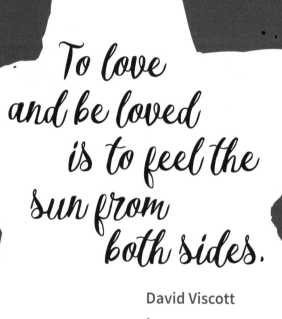

To love
and be loved
is to feel the
sun from
both sides.

David Viscott

Love... must always create sunshine, filling the hearts so full of radiance, that it overflows upon the outward world.

**Nathaniel Hawthorne**

Harmony is pure love,
for love is a concerto.

Lope de Vega

I love thee – I love thee!
Tis all that I can say;
It is my vision in the night,
My dreaming in the day.

Thomas Hood

Love consists in this, that two solitudes protect, and touch, and greet each other.

Rainer Maria Rilke

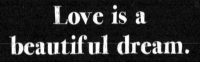

# Love is a
# beautiful dream.

William Sharp

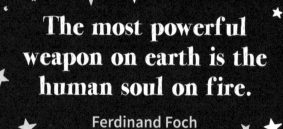

The most powerful
weapon on earth is the
human soul on fire.

Ferdinand Foch

To love abundantly is to live abundantly, and to love forever is to live forever.

Henry Drummond

The sea hath its pearls
The heaven hath its
stars; But my heart,
my heart, My heart
hath its love.

Heinrich Heine

If ever two were one,
then surely we.

Anne Bradstreet

If you're interested in finding out more
about our books, find us on Facebook
at **Summersdale Publishers** and follow
us on Twitter at **@Summersdale**.

**www.summersdale.com**